SPORTS ALL-STARS

CHRISTIAN McCAFFREY

Keith Elliot Greenberg

Lerner Publications • Minneapolis

Lerner Publications Company
An imprint of Lerner Publishing Group, Inc.
241 First Avenue North
Minneapolis, MN 55401 USA

For reading levels and more information, look up this title at www.lernerbooks.com.

Main body text set in Albany Std. Typeface provided by Agfa.

Photo Editor: Brianna Kaiser

Library of Congress Cataloging-in-Publication Data

Names: Greenberg, Keith Elliot, 1959– author.
Title: Christian McCaffrey / Keith Elliot Greenberg.
Description: Minneapolis : Lerner Publications, [2022] | Series: Sports all-stars (Lerner sports) | Includes bibliographical references and index. | Audience: Ages 7–11 | Audience: Grades 2–3 | Summary: "Carolina Panthers running back Christian McCaffrey is one of the few NFL players to record both 1,000 rushing yards and receiving yards in a single season. Read all about McCaffrey's hobbies, exercise routine, and more"— Provided by publisher.
Identifiers: LCCN 2021004104 (print) | LCCN 2021004105 (ebook) | ISBN 9781728436616 (library binding) | ISBN 9781728436685 (paperback) | ISBN 9781728436692 (ebook)
Subjects: LCSH: McCaffrey, Christian, 1996—-Juvenile literature. | Football players— United States—Biography—Juvenile literature.
Classification: LCC GV939.M2979 G74 2022 (print) | LCC GV939.M2979 (ebook) | DDC 796.332092—dc23

LC record available at https://lccn.loc.gov/2021004104
LC ebook record available at https://lccn.loc.gov/2021004105

Manufactured in the United States of America
1-49626-49556-4/21/2021

TABLE OF CONTENTS

RECORD
BREAKER

Christian McCaffrey carries the ball for the Carolina Panthers against the Jacksonville Jaguars.

Carolina Panthers running back Christian McCaffrey was ready to surprise everyone. The team was playing against the Jacksonville Jaguars on October 6, 2019.

- **Date of birth:** June 7, 1996

- **Position:** running back

- **League:** National Football League (NFL)

- **Professional highlights:** set an NFL record for catches in a season by a running back; set a record for yards gained in his first three seasons; was voted to the 2020 Pro Bowl

- **Personal highlights:** grew up in Colorado; enjoys playing the piano; received a 99 rating in *Madden NFL 21*

McCaffrey fights off a Jacksonville defender. McCaffrey's strength and speed make him hard to tackle when he runs with the ball.

Panthers quarterback Kyle Allen handed the ball to McCaffrey. Then Allen pretended to give the ball to McCaffrey's teammate, Curtis Samuel.

As some of the Jaguars ran toward Samuel, McCaffrey surged down the field. When the Jaguars realized that McCaffrey had the ball, they ran after him. They hoped to tackle McCaffrey, but no one could catch him. He kept moving until he scored a touchdown.

McCaffrey had run 84 yards to score. No Panthers player had ever run so far to score on one play. It was one of three touchdowns the 23-year-old scored that day. On one play, he leaped over a Jaguars player and landed in the end zone.

Many fans, players, and coaches thought McCaffrey was the NFL's best running back. From 2017 to 2019, he'd gained 2,920 yards as a running back and 2,523 yards as a receiver. He was the first NFL player to gain so many yards running and receiving in his first three seasons.

McCaffrey said his only goal was helping his team. Records are "cool," he said, "but it doesn't matter if you're not winning. I just want to win."

BORN TO PLAY

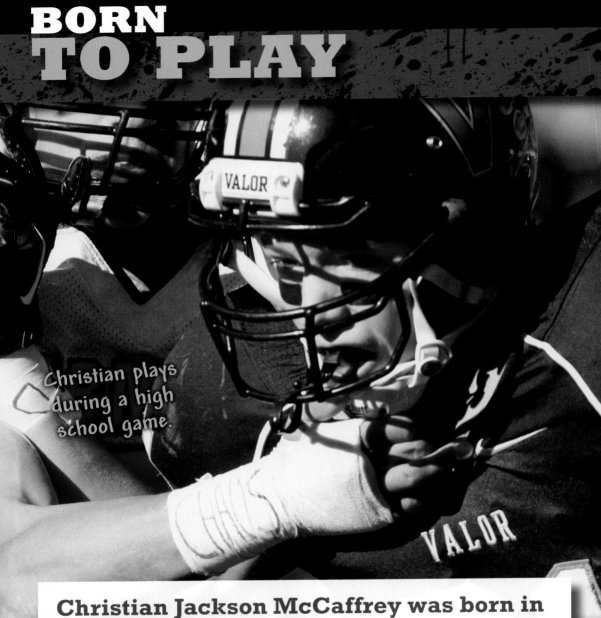

Christian plays during a high school game.

Christian Jackson McCaffrey was born in Castle Rock, Colorado, on June 7, 1996. He grew up with three brothers, Max, Dylan, and Luke. Everyone in the McCaffrey family enjoyed sports.

Christian, age five, poses for this photo with his father, Ed, and mother, Lisa.

Christian's maternal grandfather, Dave Sime, was one of the fastest people on Earth. He won a silver medal in track and field at the 1960 Summer Olympics in Rome, Italy. Christian's mother, Lisa, was a soccer star at Stanford University in California. Like her father, Dave, she was known for her speed.

Ed McCaffrey, Christian's father, played in the NFL for 13 years. As a member of the San Francisco 49ers and Denver Broncos, he won the Super Bowl three times. In 1999, the Broncos won the championship for the second year in a row. After the game, two-year-old Christian ran onto the field to celebrate with his father. A picture of Christian on the field later appeared in *Sports Illustrated* magazine.

Ed McCaffrey played in the 1998 Pro Bowl. In his NFL career, he had 565 catches and 55 touchdowns. Christian admired his father's record. "Hopefully I can catch up to him," he said.

All three of McCaffrey's brothers played football in college. Max McCaffrey played six games in the NFL with the Jaguars and 49ers.

The Valor Christian High School campus

Christian attended Valor Christian High School in Highlands Ranch, Colorado. In addition to playing running back, he starred at several other positions. He caught passes, played defense, and punted. He also played on the school's basketball team.

Christian's football teammates voted him captain of the team. But he showed no interest. "We don't need captains," he said. "We're all in this together." Instead of one leader, the team decided to have several cocaptains.

At Valor, Christian became a record-breaking running back. He set new Colorado high school records for touchdowns scored and yards gained. As a senior in 2013, Christian won the Colorado high school Player of the Year award.

   After high school, McCaffrey went to Stanford University. He didn't play much as a freshman in 2014. In 2015, he scored 13 touchdowns and won the Associated Press College Football Player of the Year award. He finished second in voting for the Heisman Trophy.

   McCaffrey scored 16 touchdowns the next season. He was ready for the NFL. After three seasons at Stanford, he entered the 2017 NFL Draft. The Panthers chose him with the eighth overall pick.

In three seasons at Stanford, McCaffrey racked up 5,128 combined rushing and receiving yards.

CHASING GREATNESS

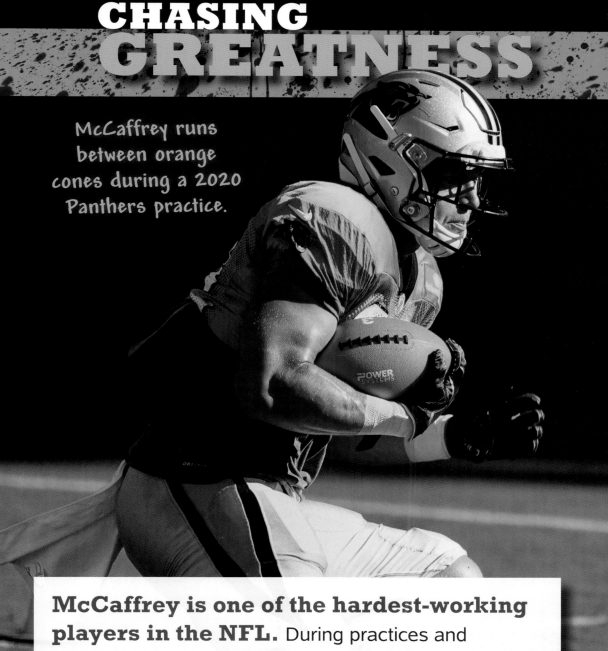

McCaffrey runs between orange cones during a 2020 Panthers practice.

McCaffrey is one of the hardest-working players in the NFL. During practices and workouts, he always gives his full effort. The work prepares him for anything that might happen in games.

"He works hard in practice and it translates to the game," teammate Shaq Thompson said.

Many reporters, coaches, and players began calling McCaffrey the NFL's top running back soon after he joined the league. The praise made him work even harder. "I think there's always things you can get better at," he said.

Ed McCaffrey taught his sons to get a lot of sleep. Growing up, none of the McCaffrey brothers stayed up late. The lesson stuck with Christian McCaffrey into his NFL years. He tries to get at least nine hours of sleep every night. Getting enough rest helps him recover from workouts more quickly.

McCaffrey eats healthful food to fuel his workouts. But sometimes he treats himself. Chips and chocolate cookies are his favorite snacks.

McCaffrey lifts 225 pounds (102 kg) above his body during a bench press exercise.

Even when it isn't football season, McCaffrey keeps working out. During the months when he isn't playing, he works out at least five days a week. One of those days is just for practicing football. The other days are for building up his muscles.

McCaffrey understands that he has to be strong to break through tackles during games. He lifts heavy weights to make all his muscles stronger. To increase his running speed, he works with track-and-field coaches. They teach him how to reach his top speed as quickly as possible. Track coaches also show McCaffrey how to turn quickly and get open to catch passes.

During games, McCaffrey stays focused. When he isn't playing or practicing, he likes to relax and have fun.

Jonathan Stewart (*left*) and McCaffrey celebrate a Carolina touchdown.

When McCaffrey joined the Panthers, he realized he had a lot in common with teammate Jonathan Stewart. Both players were talented NFL running backs. And both played the piano.

McCaffrey began playing the piano in high school. During the season, when he wants to forget about football and relax, he plays for fun. He also enjoys playing the harmonica.

Finding relaxing things to do is important to McCaffrey. In college, he enjoyed playing *Pokémon GO*. He would move around Stanford, looking at the game's map and trying to catch the game's creatures.

Pokémon GO players use mobile devices to search for the game's characters.

McCaffrey still enjoys playing video games. He has played *Madden NFL* games since he was a kid. Like most NFL players, McCaffrey is a character in the game. In *Madden NFL 21*, McCaffrey's character was one of only five players with the game's highest rating of 99.

In 2020, the new disease COVID-19 spread around the world. McCaffrey helped raise money

To prevent spreading COVID-19, McCaffrey wears a mask over his nose and mouth before a game in 2020.

to support hospital workers who risked their lives to treat patients. Hospitals used some of the money to repair lifesaving equipment.

the lives of people with Down syndrome. The foundation sets up special football camps to teach kids about teamwork and friendly competition.

At the camps, McCaffrey coaches the players and poses for photos. He says he has as much fun as the players do. Ed McCaffrey helps run the camps.

McCaffrey gives a football to a group of kids at a Panthers game. He loves to make kids smile.

McCaffrey enjoys surprising his fans. He and his father learned about Panthers fans Jeremy and Ella, a father and daughter in the US military. On Father's Day in 2020, Jeremy and Ella sat down together at a computer. Suddenly, McCaffrey and his father popped onto the screen.

Jeremy and Ella laughed with surprise when they saw Carolina's star player and his father. Christian McCaffrey told them he was proud to bring joy to people who served their country. "You guys are our heroes," Ed McCaffrey said.

McCaffrey signs an autograph for a fan before a game.

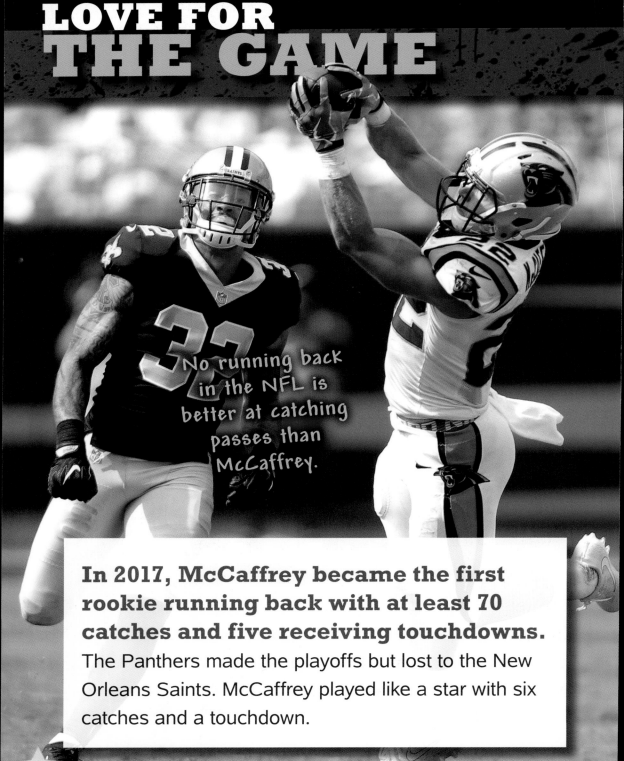

No running back in the NFL is better at catching passes than McCaffrey.

In 2017, McCaffrey became the first rookie running back with at least 70 catches and five receiving touchdowns. The Panthers made the playoffs but lost to the New Orleans Saints. McCaffrey played like a star with six catches and a touchdown.

McCaffrey breaks through a tackle during a 2018 game against the New Orleans Saints.

After a great rookie season, McCaffrey was even better in 2018. He set a record for most catches by a running back in one season with 107. He also became the first NFL player with at least 50 rushing and 50 receiving yards for five games in a row.

On December 17 against the Saints, quarterback Cam Newton handed the ball to McCaffrey. But instead of running with the ball, McCaffrey threw it. Teammate Chris Manhertz was wide open. He ran for a touchdown.

Fans couldn't believe what they had seen. McCaffrey wasn't just a great running back. For one play, he looked like a good quarterback too.

Cam Newton played for the Panthers for eight seasons.

McCaffrey looks for room to run.

In 2019, Newton was injured and played just two games. McCaffrey stepped up. For the season, he gained 1,387 rushing yards and 1,005 receiving yards. He became the third NFL player with at least 1,000 yards rushing and 1,000 yards receiving in the same season. His 116 catches broke his own NFL record. Fans, players, and coaches voted for McCaffrey to play in the Pro Bowl.

As COVID-19 spread in the summer of 2020, McCaffrey stayed close to home. He trained with his brothers. With their father watching, the brothers worked out, ran, and played football together.

The 2020 NFL season started in September. On September 20, McCaffrey was having a good game against the Tampa Bay Buccaneers. He scored his second touchdown of the game in the fourth quarter. But he hurt his ankle on the play. The injury kept him out of action for six weeks.

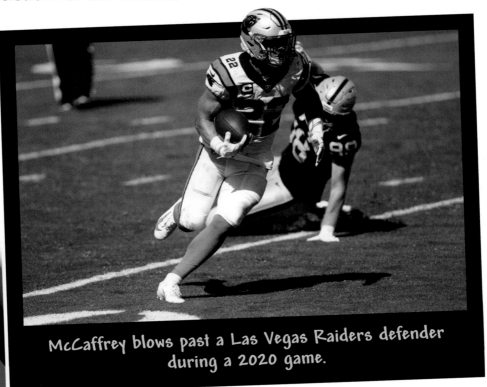

McCaffrey blows past a Las Vegas Raiders defender during a 2020 game.

When McCaffrey returned on November 8, it took about six minutes for him to score a touchdown. He scored again in the fourth quarter, but he injured his shoulder in the game. McCaffrey missed the rest of the season. It was a tough year, but he still had a bright future.

McCaffrey's skills, hard work, and love for football make him one of the NFL's biggest superstars.

"I'm going to have fun playing football, and I've really learned that I have the most success when I treat the game that way," McCaffrey said. "So I really just focus on the love for the game and having fun with my brothers on Sunday."

All-Star Stats

McCaffrey is one of the best pass-catching running backs in the NFL. But he's also a great runner. Take a look at where he ranked in NFL rushing yards in 2019.

Player	Team	Rushing yards
1. Derrick Henry	Tennessee Titans	1,540
2. Nick Chubb	Cleveland Browns	1,494
3. Christian McCaffrey	Carolina Panthers	1,387
4. Ezekiel Elliott	Dallas Cowboys	1,357
5. Chris Carson	Seattle Seahawks	1,230
6. Lamar Jackson	Baltimore Ravens	1,206
7. Leonard Fournette	Jacksonville Jaguars	1,152
8. Josh Jacobs	Oakland Raiders	1,150
9. Joe Mixon	Cincinnati Bengals	1,137
10. Dalvin Cook	Minnesota Vikings	1,135

Glossary

captain: the leader of a team

draft: when teams take turns choosing new players

end zone: the area at each end of a football field where players score touchdowns

harmonica: a small musical instrument held in the hand and played by the mouth

Heisman Trophy: an award given each year to the best player in college football

maternal: related through the mother

Pro Bowl: the NFL's all-star game

receiver: a football player whose main job is to catch passes

rookie: a first-year player

running back: a football player whose main job is running with the ball

Source Notes

7   David Newton, "Christian McCaffrey Breaks RB Receptions Record He Set Last Year," *ESPN*, December 22, 2019, https://www.espn.com/nfl/story/_/id/28353968/christian-mccaffrey-breaks-rb-receptions-record-set-last-year.

10 Bradley Smith, "'I Take Pride in Being a Complete Back': Christian McCaffrey Talks about Being the Third Player in NFL History to Join the 1000/1000 Club," Cat Scratch Reader, January 31, 2020, https://www.catscratchreader.com/2020/1/31/21116554/nfl-carolina-panthers-christian-mccaffrey-sb-nation-radio-row-miami-super-bowl-liv.

11 "Mr. Everything: Christian McCaffrey Is the Nation's Best Player, but He Can't Be Summed Up by His Achievements," *Sports Illustrated*, May 17, 2016, https://www.si.com/college/2016/05/17/mr-everything-christian-mccaffrey-nations-best-player-he-cant-be-summed-his-achievements.

14 Myles Simmons, "Panthers Sign Christian McCaffrey to Contract Extension through 2025," Panthers.com, April 16, 2020, https://www.panthers.com/news/christian-mccaffrey-contract-extension.

14 Mike Destefano, "Christian McCaffrey Talks Revamped Panthers, 'Madden' Rating, and Fantasy Football," *Complex*, August 5, 2020, https://www.complex.com/sports/2020/08/christian-mccaffrey-interview.

21 David Newton, "Christian McCaffrey and His Dad Surprise Military Family for Father's Day," *ESPN*, June 18, 2020, https://www.espn.com/blog/carolina-panthers/post/_/id/33755/christian-mccaffrey-and-his-dad-surprise-military-family-for-fathers-day.

27 Destefano, "Christian McCaffrey."

Learn More

Carolina Panthers
https://www.panthers.com

Christian McCaffrey
https://www.nfl.com/players/christian-mccaffrey/

Cooper, Robert. *The NFL Draft*. Minneapolis: Discover Roo, 2020.

Monson, James. *Behind the Scenes Football*. Minneapolis: Lerner Publications, 2020.

National Football League Facts for Kids
https://kids.kiddle.co/National_Football_League

Whiting, Jim. *The Story of the Carolina Panthers*. Minneapolis: Kaleidoscope, 2020.

Index

Photo Acknowledgments

Image credits: AP Photo/Damian Strohmeyer, pp. 4–5, 6, 21; AP Photo/Barry Gutierrez, p. 8; AP Photo/David Zalubowski, p. 9; Valor Christian High School/ Wikimedia Commons (CC 4.0), p. 11; AP Photo/Marcio Jose Sanchez, p. 12; AP Photo/Chris Carlson, p. 13; AP Photo/Perry Knotts, p. 15; AP Photo/Joe Robbins, pp. 16, 27; AP Photo/Tony Avelar, p. 17; KeongDaGreat/Shutterstock.com, p. 18; AP Photo/Brian Westerholt, pp. 19, 26; AP Photo/Bob Leverone, pp. 20, 22; AP Photo/ Jason E. Miczek, p. 23; AP Photo/Paul Jasienski, pp. 24, 25.

Cover: AP Photo/Tom DiPace.